HOYLAKE
THEN & NOW
IN COLOUR

JIM O'NEIL

First published in 2012

The History Press
The Mill, Brimscombe Port
Stroud, Gloucestershire, GL5 2QG
www.thehistorypress.co.uk

© Jim O'Neil, 2012

The right of Jim O'Neil to be identified as the Author
of this work has been asserted in accordance with the
Copyrights, Designs and Patents Act 1988.

British Library Cataloguing in Publication Data.
A catalogue record for this book is available from the British Library.

ISBN 978 0 7524 6793 1

Typesetting and origination by The History Press
Printed in India.

CONTENTS

ACKNOWLEDGEMENTS

A publication such as this cannot be done alone and it is only right to recognise everyone who has helped – apologies to any that I've inadvertently missed out.

The majority of the old photographs are from my own collection, but some have been kindly supplied by (in no particular order) Heather Chapman from Blast From The Past; Emma Keenan, Sarah Green and Lin Cooke from Hoylake Cottage Hospital; Nick Dovey and David Hirst of Burnett's Garage; and Rose Meldrum and Laurie Gartside, former local residents. Heather Chapman and John Parr (Hoylake Lifeboat Museum) have also been very helpful on dates.

Special mention must be given to Barbara, Dave and John Caine of Max Spielmann's Hoylake branch for processing the films and reprints fast and efficiently – a perfect combination of a national chain and a family concern.

The massive job of actually converting the old images into a format fit for the twenty-first century has been handled beautifully by Marianthi Lainas, my secretary, who also typed several thousand words of deathless prose.

I am of course grateful to all the staff at The History Press, especially Jessica Andrews, my editor, for commissioning the book and handling endless queries, and to Chris West for the cover design.

Thank you all!

ABOUT THE AUTHOR

Jim O'Neil is descended from IRA gun-runners on his father's side and Spanish pirates on his mother's side – the family name being Cornelius – which probably goes a long way to explain his rather unusual views on local history and life in general. He was born in Heswall and only three days later moved to Greasby. Both are historic villages in Wirral and they endeared him to the peninsula forever.

After three years teacher training at Chester College and at Plattsburgh University, USA, he suddenly found that he was married and living in Hoylake. Having recovered from the shock, he promised himself never to move house again and so far has managed to keep that promise.

He currently works part-time for three employers, including teaching local history to adult students in an informal setting for Wirral 3Ls. His other jobs are collecting and redistributing unwanted paint (the Community RePaint Wirral scheme), proof-reading brochures and playing the church organ.

He has written extensively on the local history of the Wirral but this is his first hardback book and he plans to live long enough to write rather more of them.

INTRODUCTION

Somehow seventeen years have passed, almost to the day, since I wrote the introduction to my earlier book *West Kirby to Hoylake* and yet I find that some words I wrote then are just as relevant now:

'... even the last fifteen years have seen vast changes in the fortunes of Hoylake, to an extent which the older residents could never have predicted. Change is a constant process, without which stagnation can set in, but change for its own sake can cause untold loss of the heritage of a town... demolition is irreversible.'

That publication was reprinted in 2006 with some corrections to the captions but the slow yet inevitable processes of both physical change and continuing research have led to this new publication. So what has changed? First and foremost, it gratifying to record that, after intense local and national pressure, the fight to keep our excellent and recently refurbished public library has been won, and indeed the victory has set a national legal precedent.

Another positive change is that Hoylake hosted the Open Golf Championship in 2006, which enabled much of the south-west end of Market Street to be overhauled; it is planned that the 2014 Open will also be here in Hoylake, which will hopefully make the renovation of the rest of the street and the promenade financially viable.

The former Hoylake Parade School is now a thriving community centre, there is a plan for the old toilet block to be converted into a café, the new lifeboat station stands proudly on the site of the fondly-remembered open-air swimming pool and the old lifeboat station is being turned into a lifeboat museum – sometimes change is indeed for the better!

Spending a day taking the new photographs to precisely mirror the old views was really enjoyable and amazingly instructive – not as many as I thought were taken from the middle of the road but on a few occasions it did get a bit scary! It soon became clear that the old-time photographers were very skilled, very patient and had some excellent lenses.

It was hard to limit the number of photographs I chose, Hoylake and Meols being beloved of Victorian and Edwardian photographers during the heyday of the area as a holiday resort. I also found that sometimes I needed relatively tiny details, such as a concrete moulding or single coping stone to line up the pictures accurately. Strangely, however, the biggest problem actually turned out to be the trees – obviously people took photographs of their proud new buildings and included the neat gardens and shrubs, which, a century on, have grown significantly and simply block the view.

If there is a moral to this tale, it's this: go find, look and enjoy – and if you have a camera, please use it to help record and preserve the Hoylake we all know and love.

Jim O'Neil, Hoylake, 2011

WELCOME TO HOYLAKE!

THIS BOOK WILL take you on a journey of discovery from Little Meols (now Meols Drive to Lake Place) through Hoose (now central Hoylake to Carlton Lane) finishing in Great Meols (now just called Meols). It should open your eyes to some of the changes that have taken place over the last 120 years, with some surprises to be seen along the way. Bring a magnifying glass – you'll be glad you did! So, let our journey begin, with not a car in sight! It's not easy nowadays to remember that these roads were originally built for people and animals to walk along. The buildings and the trees date the photograph on the right to early spring, probably in 1898 or 1899.

THE PERCEIVED WISDOM in Hoylake is that the famous local writer and historian the Revd Dr Charles William Budden, who lived at No. 1 Market Street in the first decades of the twentieth century, owned the first motorcar in Hoylake – although I feel that it would be really unfair to blame all our modern traffic problems on just one man! With traffic comes white lines, yellow lines, signs, bollards and, of course, roundabouts. In 2005 a public consultation was held to tell everyone what was to happen to this particular roundabout (left). The sculpture on the roundabout is called Knot of Knots and was designed by David Annand. A descriptive poem by Elizabeth Davey is on a plinth, just off the photograph to the right, with a miniature copy of part of the sculpture – rather safer to stand and stare at!

TURNING IN

A FEW YEARS later, and summer flowers can now be seen in tubs by the 'big lamp' (as it was known) and the flowerbeds have been laid out in front of The Quadrant. This was really the 'posh' end of Hoylake, with large houses, banks, Hoylake Town Hall and, in the middle distance on the right, the Market Hall, which was built in 1901. This postcard was mailed on 28 August 1911,

showing that traffic problems are not a new phenomenon (the cyclists are riding on the wrong side of the road and the delivery van is on the pavement!) and also giving an indication as to roughly when the photograph was taken.

THERE IS STILL a vehicle parked outside The Quadrant – but it *is* in a designated parking bay! Market Street takes its name from the Market Hall, which has long since been renamed Central Hall; The Quadrant is so named because of the shape of the building. It is really only in the last ten years that the established businesses in that block have changed – to us as local residents it has always seemed that the NatWest Bank, the Midland Bank, Kingsley's Auction Room and the various local and national governmental offices were part of the very fabric of the town. New businesses such as wine bars, street cafés, opticians and florists have moved in and given it new life.

BUILDINGS TO IMPRESS

KING'S GAP HOYLAKE.

THE YEARS ROLL on: the 'big lamp' was replaced by the roundabout in 1937 and the need for white lane markings show that traffic was growing. The style of the old photograph (from a Christmas card) suggests that it was taken around the 1950s. The large building in the centre was the Stanley Hotel, which was named after the landowners, the Stanley family of Hooton and Alderley, who also gave their name to Stanley Road. The Stanley family were great benefactors to the town, contributing, for example, to the cost of the Institute, later to become the YMCA.

SINCE OUR OLD photograph, the Stanley Hotel has been replaced by Montrose Court but the original boundary wall has been retained.

11

THE CONGREGATIONAL CHURCH

LOOKING SOUTH-EAST across Meols Drive, this thatched cottage stood on the edge of the site of the Congregational church. The original is, unfortunately, not clear enough to allow us to name the person in the doorway, but he or she was possibly a member of the Roach family. The two small windows just visible on the left are from a building that dates from 1884 (now the church hall), which gives us an earliest date that this photograph could have been taken. The church itself was completed in 1906, which gives us a latest date for the photograph.

HOYLAKE CHAPEL NOW stands on this site, and the trees hide the gable end of the house on the right. The two windows on the far left of the old photograph can only just about be seen in the modern picture.

BOMBED OUT

HOYLAKE CONGREGATIONAL CHURCH, on the corner of Station Road, was designed by John Douglas of Chester and was completed in 1906. The spire, most of the roof and the excellent First World War memorial window were destroyed by German incendiary bombs during the night of 20 December 1940; most of the damage was done by just one bomb, which jammed

itself in one of the ventilation spaces at the top of the spire. The building was open to the elements and virtually unusable until 1950, so that church services, a servicemen's canteen, an overflow sorting office and various other wartime functions all had to be accommodated in the hall – I've no idea how they managed it! This postcard was mailed on 26 August 1912.

AS WITH MANY of the photographs in this book, the trees have grown tall and wide, partly obscuring the building. In 1950 the pieces of stained glass were all painstakingly repaired and today the window is looking even more historically interesting, in the sense that there are far more pieces of black lead than a stained-glass artist would normally have used; these are where the cracks have been extremely well repaired, and they take a while to spot. The spire was never replaced. The building became Hoylake URC in 1972 and was sold to Hoylake Chapel in 1992. Today Station Road is the main access to both the railway station and the adjoining industrial estate, so the new pedestrian refuges are a welcome addition!

ST HILDEBURGH'S CHURCH

ORIGINALLY BUILT AS a chapel of ease, St Hildeburgh's Church of England church in Stanley Road (right) was designed by Edmund Kirby of Liverpool. Construction began in September 1897 and, although not quite completed, it was opened for worship on 1 May 1899. It was consecrated on 7 September 1899 and became the parish church of Hoylake in 1976, when Holy Trinity church was demolished. The building on the far left was known as The King's Gap Court Hotel until earlier this year.

IT IS SIMPLY not possible to take precisely this view today. The boundary wall in the front of the old photograph is in fact still there, adjoining the public footpath which runs between the church and the vicarage and onward across the golf course. However, time has transformed the few small bushes growing behind the wall into a huge thicket of trees and I really did not want to just print a green rectangle here! I *have* included the fencing behind the pillar box on the left as it shows the building site where the hotel is being refurbished and extended as the latest Holiday Inn.

SPORTING TIMES

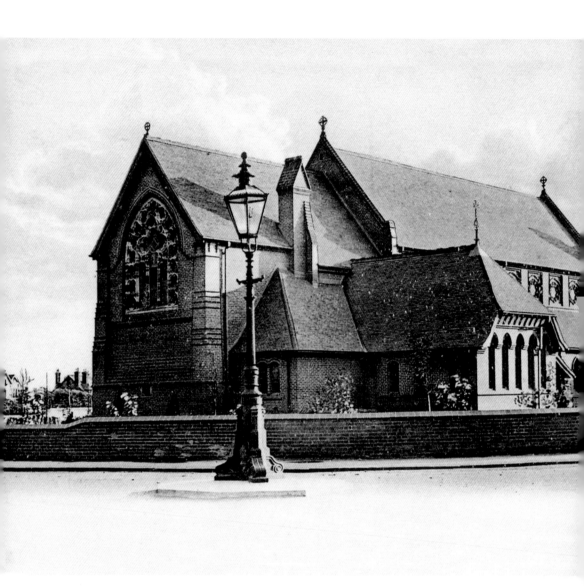

IN 1914 LOCAL historian Charles Roberts wrote '... where St Hildeburgh's church now stands was an old bowling green with a wall round and a pavilion of a kind upon it, in which it is said more drink was consumed than in the Green Lodge Hotel opposite.' We are in the heart of the old country gentry sporting area; the bowling green was part of the Hoylake Racecourse, the races being held between 1840 and 1876. The eighteenth-century medical craze for bathing in the sea was catered for at the end of the road at Red Rocks. Today there is the Royal Liverpool Golf Club, and slightly further inland is Hoylake Municipal Golf Course.

THESE PHOTOGRAPHS ARE taken in King's Gap, facing into Stanley Road on the right. King's Gap is so called because it is supposed to mark the route that King William III took in 1690 to Hoyle Lake when he sailed from his anchorage there on his royal expedition to Ireland, following the disastrous government expedition of 1689. Precisely which piles of sand his horse picked his way through we can never know, but it must have been around here somewhere!

HERE TO STAY

HERE IS ANOTHER interesting quote from Charles Roberts written in 1914 and referring to a period fifty years earlier:

We must draw attention to the 'Green Lodge Hotel', situated in Stanley Road and immediately opposite to the principal entrance of the Racecourse. The Green Lodge is one of the oldest and best known hotels in Wirral. The Lodge for quite a generation was in the hands of the Ball family, and 'Old John'. 'Young John' and the son-in-law, Peter Theopholus Evans, sharing the continuous tenancy between them. At the time it was not so large as at present, a new wing having been added after Mr. Evans' death. During the occupation of Mr. Evans it was chiefly a family residential hotel, and was much frequented by well-to-do families from Liverpool. It was also a rendezvous for Sunday afternoon teas, many people journeying along the shore from New Brighton, or else driving by road to the Lodge for tea, which had then a well-known reputation.

Sources vary as to the age of the Green Lodge, but it most likely dates from 1750. The photograph below is certainly the oldest I have seen, possibly dating from the 1890s.

TAKEN IN 2011, the modern view on the left shows the 'new wing' mentioned by Charles Roberts. The building is looking well maintained, with the addition of hanging baskets and outdoor seating.

SHOWING THE WAY

THERE HAVE BEEN two lighthouses at Hoylake since as early as 1764 to guide ships through the treacherous sandbanks and shifting channels around the north Wirral coast and into Liverpool. They were part of a system of lighthouses all along the Wirral shore, which navigators would

use by lining them up in pairs to know when to change course to reach Liverpool safely. This is the Upper Lighthouse in Valentia Road, photographed early in the twentieth century. It was built in 1865–6 and last lit on 14 May 1886. There is a tiny 'hidden' entrance to a tunnel in the front garden.

THE GATEPOST SHOWN in the old photograph is the left-hand post in the modern picture – which was taken from the only suitable gap in the trees! The main gates have been replaced by a brick wall, clearly some time ago, and the railings have been replaced with fencing panels. The present owners of the lighthouse are working on a careful restoration of the building, and their Christmas light displays have to be seen to be believed!

THE 'IRON MONSTER'

THE ARRIVAL OF the 'iron monster' at Hoylake on 18 January 1866 was the main catalyst for the transformation of Hoylake from a playground for the rich into a holiday destination for the masses. It started a snowball effect – visitors arriving by train led to shops and boarding houses, which led to speculative building of houses to rent, which led to building of houses for sale, which led to more shops, and so on. Writing in 1914, Charles Roberts records that the first railway station building

was 'an old light-coloured [wooden] structure [which was] superceded some years ago by the present [i.e. second] building.' No photographs are known to exist of the first station building that he mentions; this view of the second building on the Liverpool-bound platform dates from about 1900.

THE MODERN VIEW above was taken from the level crossing on Station Road, from that point renamed Carr Lane, and is the extremely busy access road to both the industrial estate and a housing estate. There is a train in each direction every fifteen minutes and a new Park & Ride car park, providing an excellent service for commuters and day trippers travelling in both directions! The railway line was electrified from 14 March 1938, at which time the new Manor Road station opened.

ARRIVING
IN STYLE

THE RAILWAY WAS extended from Hoylake to West Kirby on 1 April 1878 but it was still only single-track; the line was double-tracked as far as Hoylake from 1 June 1895, the section to West Kirby being double-tracked in 1896. The effect on West Kirby was just as dramatic as it had been on Hoylake – in fact it created a whole new village centre, the original West Kirby today being known as the 'Old Village'. This photograph, showing 'Locomotive No. 11' arriving at the West Kirby-bound platform at Hoylake station, is from a postcard mailed on 31 August 1906, effectively dating it to within ten years.

THE MORE DISCERNING reader will quickly realise that the photographer of the older picture was looking slightly downwards onto the station (the top

surface of the platform is visible). It could not have been taken from the present footbridge at that time, as it was not built until nearly forty years later, but looking at the alignment of the platform as seen here, it was probably taken from the signal box, which was demolished in December 1994. The chimney and the gasometers have all gone, but the large industrial estate is still working.

ART DECO IN HOYLAKE

THE WIRRAL RAILWAY became part of the London, Midland and Scottish Railway (LMS) on 1 January 1923. These photographs show the present (third) Hoylake station; the architect may have been influenced by Charles Holden's London Transport stations. It was designed in the architects' section of the office of W.K. Wallace, the chief civil engineer to the LMS, as part of the

electrification scheme, which came into use on 14 March 1938. The line became part of British Rail in 1948, giving a guide to the date of the picture.

THE ONLY MAJOR change over the years has been that the LMS sign has been replaced by the Merseyrail sign. The modern 'through stations' used in the Hornby Dublo railway sets in the 1930s were modelled on this striking art deco building. It is now a listed building, although I am left wondering how many people actually really look at it – they should, it is a real architectural gem! It has also been adapted to meet modern disability access rules, with the ticket office counter being movable and a modern toilet installed, both achieved without damaging the design in any way.

THE QUADRANT

RETURNING TO MARKET Street, these flowerbeds, the pride and joy of the Hoylake UDC Parks and Gardens Department, were a favourite of local photographers for many years. Oh so 'municipal', no walking on the grass or sitting by the flowers was allowed (you had to sit on the benches provided outside the railings). It is clearly half-past eleven on a lovely summer's morning in the old photograph on the right – but what was the year? Although this particular card was not posted, the required postage, the single-decker bus and the women's clothing all suggest the mid-1930s.

WHERE HAVE ALL the flowers gone? – or did someone already sing that? (See page 63 for the answer). More importantly, where have all the banks (and building societies) gone? Earlier this year, our last remaining bank, the HSBC, deserted Hoylake in favour of the over-endowed and rather competitive atmosphere of West Kirby. Fortunately, we have an excellent post office, open six days a week. We do also have new bench seats in this part of Market Street but strangely they all face away from the long, attractive street view.

HOYLAKE TOWN HALL

HOYLAKE, OF COURSE, could never be considered a town without a town hall. Construction of
Hoylake Town Hall began in February 1897 and it was officially opened on 2 February 1898.
On 1 April 1974 Hoylake UDC was abolished and slowly the services available to the public were
removed to Wallasey Town Hall. Soon afterwards a relatively small internal fire on the first floor
damaged a few floor beams and some panelling in what was the original council chamber.

HOYLAKE TOWN HALL stood empty and forlorn for several years. Meanwhile, the Jobcentre's
fifty-year lease of The Priory in Meols Drive ran out in 1998. They had problems trying to
find new premises until finally, on 9 February 1999, Alan Whitehead from their Salford office

quite unexpectedly knocked on my door to ask for suggestions. Who sent him to me or why will probably forever remain a mystery. Anyway, it proved to be a fruitful move for all concerned as I immediately took him up to the town hall where local entrepreneur Tony Crane was masterminding the restoration and the rest, as they say, is history. It is now known as Hoylake Jobcentreplus and must rate as one of the most architecturally important Jobcentres in the UK.

LET'S GO SHOPPING

IN 1994 I wrote: 'A view beloved of photographers for over a century, but I make no apologies for including it as I consider it the best I have seen.' The detail is excellent – note especially the lady lifting her skirt to avoid the piles of horse-droppings all along the road! On the rear of the horse-drawn van can be seen an advertisement for 'Harry Eccles & Co., The Stores, Hoylake'. In 1905 this company had shops at No. 42 Market Street and No. 18 Birkenhead Road. The van also mentions that they were 'Tea, Coffee & Provision Dealers' and 'Importers of Finest Irish Butters'.

NOW WHEN I came to try to take the exact same view, I realised what an incredible photograph I was looking at – the modern view on the left is only just over half of the original width! There is just one piece of the arcading left today and I'm pleased to see that it has been restored. I have now also realised how tricky these arcades make any access to the upper floors – you need to remove the glass panels on top of the ironwork to let a ladder through to the wall.

WHAT WE HAVE LOST

THIS BEAUTIFUL THATCHED cottage, probably built in the late eighteenth or early nineteenth century, belonged to the Barlow family. Before the railway arrived Hoose was just a small fishing village (it was not even taxable in the Domesday survey of 1086), and this would have been typical of the buildings in the area right up to the early nineteenth century. It can be clearly identified on

the first edition of the 25-inch Ordnance Survey plan, surveyed in 1871. However, by the time the second edition was published in 1897, it had been demolished to make way for Wood Street.

THIS IS PROBABLY the most dramatically-changed pair of photographs in the book! Today the centre of Hoose is high-density terraced houses for working men – and having lived in one for thirty-six years I can thoroughly recommend them! This road was originally meant to be called Barlow Street, which would have had some meaning, rather than Wood Street, which would not, since there were hardly any trees in the area. However, it was named Wood Street by an owner of one of the adjacent properties, who also owned properties in Wood Street in Liverpool. Facing us in the distance, the white door next to the jigger was the home of Chris Boardman in 1992, when he won his Olympic Gold Medal for cycling – and that night the Union Flag banners were all over the road!

THE CORNER SHOP

MANY OF THE side roads off Market Street, such as Rudd Street, Grove Road and Lake Place, had small corner businesses, many of which have gone over the last forty years, partly due to changing shopping habits and partly due to increased living space. Shaw Street, for example, had four corner shops in 1975 – now it has one. The old photograph below shows No. 19 Wood Street at the junction with Walker Street sometime around the First World War, judging by the clothes. This was John Smith's dairy shop, but the actual dairy was at New Farm, off Carr Lane. The boy with

the bicycle on the left is Bill Rowlands, John Smith is by the horse, and George Beamer is on the cart. The names of the small children are not known.

IT WAS USUALLY the case that the dairy and the shop were actually together – the author's house in Shaw Street being a dairy for many years, with a connecting door to the corner shop at the end of the terrace; the dairy has left us a few internal architectural oddities and the shop next door lasted until only some thirty years ago. At first glance it is easy to miss features on buildings such as this diagonal corner but once seen they are obvious and the same feature can be spotted on many corners. Forty years ago there were very few cars in these streets after the shops closed; today these streets are parked up solidly every night, with the ubiquitous working man's white van a popular feature!

SHOPPING FOR EVERYONE

J. HASKINS & SONS had two shops, this one at No. 76 Market Street, where the Co-op stands today, and one in Grange Road, West Kirby. In 1905 the firm was described as 'golf club and ball makers, hairdressers and tobacconists'. In the old photograph, taken around the 1920s, 'Pop' Haskins stands on the left, and on the right is George Whitely, Pop's son-in-law. Next to this shop stood a whole row of shops built in what seems to have been a similar style but which never seemed to feature much in photographs – it was always in the distance or end-on and never really photographed in its own right.

THE CO-OP BUILDING is the modern equivalent of J. Haskins & Sons, although the signage is not nearly as detailed! The bricks forming the foundation of the front wall of Haskins' shop were exposed in 2006 when the pavement was re-laid. Adjoining this site today is a block of shops simply called 'The Row', which is perfectly functional, with living accommodation above and car parking and loading bays behind, but totally lacking in architectural style or beauty.

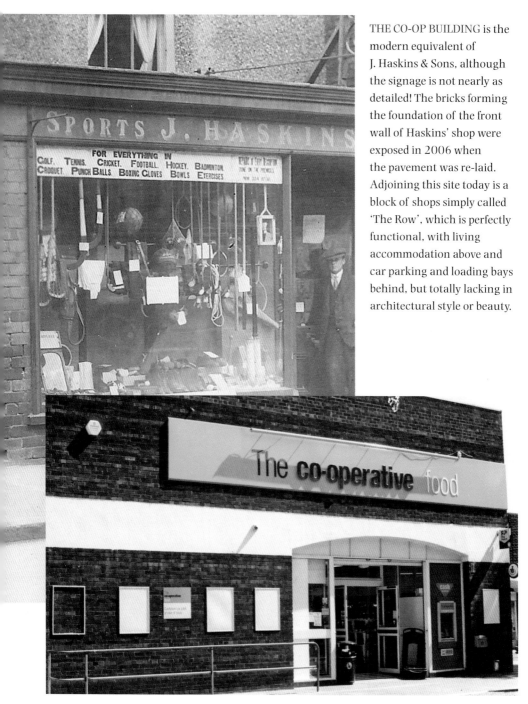

TIME FOR A DRINK

THE PRINCIPAL BUSINESS HOUSE O

SHIP INN, HOYLAKE.

A. SM
PRO

Birkenhead Brewery's Beautiful Sparkling Beers only.

Estimates for Party Catering. Free Char-a-Banc Park.

SHIP INN

R.A.O.B

TEL. 319

Spend your Holiday in Hoylake—3 miles Promenade, lovely Sc

'THE PRINCIPAL BUSINESS house of Hoylake' as defined, presumably, by Alfred Smith himself, is listed in the *Hawling's Directory* of about 1923, which confirms the sort of date that the clothing, the charabanc and the open-top car all suggest. The idea of diversification in business is nothing new: charabancs such as the one shown here were often really only in use at weekends and on bank holidays. The bodies with the seats were detachable and during the working week a truck body with sides or a flat-bed body would be used. Then a crane would be used to replace the seats on the Friday evening. I really can't imagine that idea meeting health and safety regulations today!

TO ANY HOYLAKE resident the photograph below hardly needs the words 'Ship Inn' but it is only when you compare the present view in detail you realise just how much it has changed – windows, doors, roof lines etc. Notice particularly the extension on the left, added since the earlier drawing, but also changed again since being built – the extra doorway is now blocked up. Today the Ship Inn is very much part of the community and hosts music nights, quizzes and barbecues to name but a few activities. Note the disability scooter parked outside – today Hoylake is still popular as a dormitory settlement but it also has a generally aging population.

HOYLAKE.

HEADQUARTERS OF THE

Hoylake United F.C.;
Hoylake Central Bowling Green.
Hilbre Lodge R.A.O.B.—Thursday, 7-30.
Char-a-Banc Trips every day for Wales & Wirral—
Safe, Clean Sands for Children.

and Sunshine.

MARKET STREET

THIS VIEW OF Market Street
has Shaw Street on the right and
Sycamore Grove (known locally as
'Cockle Alley') on the extreme left.
As with so many of the photographs
of this era (the card was posted on
19 September 1908) it is the total
lack of clutter that amazes me – no
litter bins or A-boards or cars parked
on the pavement or even on the
road! The pulled-down blinds show
that it was taken during opening
hours, and I would guess about
midday with an overcast sky as
there are no shadows.

I TOOK THE modern picture
from slightly to the right of the

old photograph, partly to show where the pavement was re-aligned in the 1930s and partly to make sure that my life wasn't put in danger! The right side of the main road is virtually unchanged but there are at least three phases of rebuilding evident on the left. The tall gable end with the finial, just left of centre, marks the corner of Melrose Avenue, formerly known as Cross Street, which was named after the builder.

LOOKING BACK

THIS PHOTOGRAPH IS taken from virtually
the same position as the last one, just facing
the opposite way (here Shaw Street is on the
left). The Punch Bowl, shown here in about the
1920s, is the second of that name on the site.
No photographs of the first building are known,
but Charles Roberts, writing in about 1914,
describes the older building as '... the oldest public
house in the village, kept and owned by Robert
Shaw; it was not the Punch Bowl of today, for
it then consisted of a small thatched building,
with little accommodation, whilst the front,
facing Market Street, were stables which have
been converted into its present and more suitable
business condition.' Looking at the photograph
suggests that it is slightly later, perhaps when the

converted stables had been completely rebuilt. It would also seem likely that Robert Shaw gave his name to Shaw Street, although in the nineteenth century the land was owned by John Ralph Shaw of Arrowe Hall, so it is hard to be sure.

THE ANGLE OF the second building made this part of Market Street relatively narrow and as early as 1918 it was acknowledged that there was a traffic problem, but it was nearly twenty years before the present (third) Punch Bowl was built in 1936 and the pavement was cut back to its current position. The small bread shop far left has gone and the site is now occupied by Hoylake Library, set back and parallel to the road.

47

HOLY TRINITY CHURCH

THE FOUNDATION STONE for Holy Trinity church in Church Road was laid on 9 April 1832, and the building was consecrated on 1 November 1833. It was built to accommodate both the local fishermen and the large number of summer visitors, much of the funding coming from an appeal issued to the merchants of Liverpool, many of whom lived in Hoylake. It became the parish church of Hoylake in 1860. The closest I have been able to date this photograph is between 1900 and 1914.

BY 1914 CHARLES Roberts was able
to state that 'The present generation
appear to have been crowded out,
and now worship in the Bethel,
a small building at the bottom of
Church Road [Trinity Road] where
services on Sunday evenings are
regularly held with, we believe, a
good attendance of the fishermen
and their families.' That building
still stands and is now a car repair
garage. I really like the modern
photograph above, which shows just
how much the trees have grown,
sheltering the parish graveyard, a
lovely rural oasis of peace bounded
by walls made from the warm, red
local sandstone.

CHURCH VIEW

THE HOUSES ON the extreme right in the right-hand photograph are in Trinity Road – a terraced block still called Church View – well, it *was* in about 1885 when they built it! Holy Trinity church was demolished in 1976, due to a combination of all the usual reasons – falling membership numbers, maintenance costs, and so on – but at least one part was saved – the bell went to a church in Cheshire.

I SUSPECT THAT many readers dreamed of winning fortunes on Vernon's Pools in pre-National Lottery days. Vernon Sangster's remains are one of many buried in the large oval space where the church once stood. The graveyard also includes two winners of the VC, two *Lusitania* graves, one *Titanic* grave and more recently one *Piper Alpha* disaster grave. Church View still stands looking over this typically English scene.

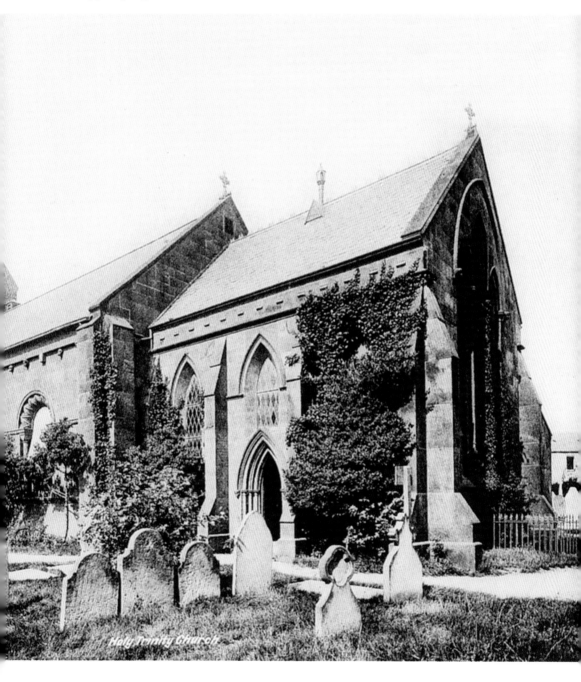

SCHOOL LANE, HOYLAKE

SCHOOL LANE, HOYLAKE, with the back wall of the graveyard on the right, seen sometime in the early 1950s, judging by the clothes (the lady pushing the pram has a 1950s dress and the lady in

the road wears 1940s attire). There seems to be two children in the pram, the nearer child being slightly older – where are they now, I wonder? The small shop on the left was a favourite of local schoolchildren as the original church school was nearby. The school is just out of sight on the right, at the end of the wall.

THE BUILDING ON the left is just about recognizable but the rest of the lane has changed beyond all recognition. In this view the brick building centre left is the last remaining part of a rather utilitarian block of flats called Hoose Court, the bulk of which was demolished whilst I was planning this book in June 2011. The old name for central Hoylake, Hoose is a derivation of *hulse*, meaning 'hills' (as in 'sandhills'), and is still the name of the electoral ward. The site of the flats is now cleared and there was a very succesful public consultation by Wirral Partnership Homes in October 2011 to ask local people for ideas for re-developing the area.

HOYLAKE OLD AND EVEN OLDER!

I FEEL THAT this picture should really be re-named 'Hoylake Old & Even Older'! The shop on the extreme left of the drawing is one of a block which still survives, now used by two financial services companies. The next building, behind the low stone wall, was a bakery, and Hoylake Library now stands on the site. In the far centre distance is the chimney stack and roof of the former sub-post office, this roof and gable end being just visible in the photograph below. The arched structure next to it was built in 1915 as the Central Garage, later renamed the

Hoylake
Old & New
John Pride

Kingsway Garage, and was converted into the Wirral Horn Arcade in September 1979. The whole of the next block was demolished and replaced by the Blue Anchor. The final building on the right is now Hoylake Fisheries, which itself has long had a replacement doorway. Internal and external evidence both suggest a date of about 1939 for this drawing.

THE WIRRAL HORN Arcade was demolished in 2007 and replaced by the new block of ground-floor shops and offices, including Kingsleys Auction Room, situated for many years in The Quadrant. This new block has living accommodation on the first floor and the building bears the baffling datestone 'ROCKLIS THEA 2008' – I have been unable to find anyone who knows what it means!

MEET THE LOCALS

THIS BUILDING WAS known as Bird's Terrace, named after Richard Bird, and is seen above around 1900. It was demolished to make way for Kingsway Cinema, which opened on 10 July 1915.

Charles Roberts, writing in about 1914, comments 'Bird's yard has now been demolished, a cinema being erected on the Front, whilst no doubt, the land at the back will be put to some useful purpose. The cinema will prove a big attraction and ornament to the main street.'

THE CINEMA LASTED forty-five years, closing on 12 March 1960, and was then demolished to make way for the building that is now occupied by Home Bargains. The adjoining block of cottages still stand on almost exactly the same alignment as Bird's Terrace, as evidenced by the 1909 edition of the 25-inch Ordnance Survey plan.

HORSE POWER

WE HAVE MOVED about one hundred yards in the same direction along Market Street from the photograph on page 47. This is another of those views which shows one side virtually unchanged, the other totally different. My 'original' of this photograph has been coloured in by hand; the photograph was probably first put on sale in black and white, then later re-issued in 'colour' to increase sales. The tall building in the distance on the left is the YMCA, which was built in 1904, and the clothes suggest the photograph was taken no later than the First World War. Personally, I feel quite sorry for the horse!

THE CAR PARK sign shows where the second building on the right in the above picture used to stand – the one with the bay window and the lower roof line. This was the Lighthouse Inn, a really small beer house. In the Victorian period it was easy to get a license: all that was needed was for two resident ratepayers to sign a requisition to the relevant government department and enclose the small fee and then a licence would be sent. I did not try to re-enact the people posing – they are precisely in line with the car park entrance!

WALKING OUT

ESSENTIALLY THE SAME view as seen in the previous pair of images, but this old photograph is taken looking in the opposite direction and slightly later. The soldier standing proudly by the pram, 'walking out' with what just had to be his wife in those days, appears to be in First World War

Market Street. Hoylake MM   36   E.R.J's WIR. GREASBY

uniform, but quite why they are carefully wending their way between the piles of horse-droppings instead of using the wide, clean pavement I have no idea! Frustratingly, it is possible to see that the poster on the right is advertising a lecture of some sort, but the date is just too small to make out! The wall on the right is the boundary of the Congregational chapel.

THE NEW BLOCK on the right replaces the former Congregational chapel on the corner of Chapel Road. The other buildings on the right in the photograph above have all long gone. The tall gable on the left, which is now painted white, is the old village school, now converted into individual cottages. (Incidentally, Chapel Road took its name from another building a little way along the road and not from this chapel.) This corner is the point where Market Street changes name and becomes Birkenhead Road.

A ROAD BY ANY OTHER NAME

THE OLD PHOTOGRAPH on the right can be dated to sometime between 1904, when the Institute was built (just visible on the left), and 1910, when Hoylake Cottage Hospital was erected (in this photograph the site is still sand hills). The workman on the left has unconsciously struck the pose of workmen everywhere: leaning on his shovel! In the foreground Chapel Road is on the left, and Hoyle Road is on the left in the middle distance. The block of shops on the right runs between Lee Road and Newton Road, but the gable end in the middle distance on the right is Manor Road; the block of shops that now stands between

Newton Road and Manor Road had not yet been built. Notice the wonderful telegraph poles, which even had decorative finials on the top.

NOW WE HAVE the 'missing' block of shops, far right, but the metal arcading has all gone. The modern photograph on the left highlights how flower power is blooming all along Market Street, Birkenhead Road, the Promenade and the various parks and open spaces. These planters and flowerbeds are part of a magnificent ongoing effort by the Friends of Hoylake & Meols in Bloom, a local voluntary group. Long may they flourish!

YMCA

AN ARTIST'S IMPRESSION of the planned Hoylake Institute, from a postcard posted on 19 December 1903. The comment on the bottom, which is dated 12 December 1903, reads 'Total takings for three days £603 – this is good work – & we hope to clear £550 for the Institute. It has been hard work all through.' The foundation stone was laid by Lord and Lady Stanley of Alderley on 20 July 1904. The building was of Ruabon bricks, with stone facings and Welsh slates. The cost, including furniture, was about £6,000. The premises were opened on 16 December 1904 by the Mayor of Liverpool. In October 1912 Messrs. George Fenton and Victor Branford leased the Institute for use as a cinema until at least July 1915, some sources stating 1919.

PROPOSED HOYLAKE INSTITUTE.

THE BUILDING WAS taken over by the YMCA in 1921 and in 1936–7 the basketball team were All-England Champions and represented England at the Paris Exposition in 1937. Apart from the section on the left, which is now Hoylake Evangelical church, the building was demolished in 1986. At that time an appeal was set up to raise money for a commemorative stone and I put a

'mock-up' on display in his shop window to support the appeal. The stone was erected outside the present building, Elmtree Court, on 30 October 1987. The design of the building well reflects the look of the surrounding buildings.

HOYLAKE COTTAGE
HOSPITAL

HOYLAKE COTTAGE HOSPITAL, with Deneshey Road on the left. The hospital began in temporary premises in 1906 in Church Road, which is now called Trinity Road. The present building opened

in 1910 but it soon became clear that it would have to be extended. In 1914 a 'Shilling Fund' was started and it raised £14,018. (A shilling was the equivalent coin to the modern 5 pence piece.) Here we see the hospital with the extensions on each side that were completed in 1928.

TO TAKE PRECISELY the same view today would have required several factors to fall into place at the same time – sunlight at the correct angle, access to an upper floor of one of the buildings across Market Street and much shorter trees! However, this photograph compares well. The hospital is in the throes of a major rebuild and extension, as evidenced by the fencing and the scaffolding poles on the right, and various earlier minor changes, such as those to the main entrance, can clearly be seen.

BURNETT'S GARAGE

MANY LONG-TIME residents of Hoylake will recall Burnett's Garage with a touch of nostalgia as the place where they bought their first car. Burnett's was established in the 1920s and stood on Birkenhead Road directly opposite what was to become the top of Deneshey Road. By the

1970s it was regularly selling 100 new cars a year. This site was sold to a petrol company in 1987, but Burnett's is still very much in business on the Carr Lane industrial estate.

TODAY THERE IS a petrol station on the site, opposite Deneshey Road. The two houses on the left are now Nos 50 and 52 Birkenhead Road (the continuation of Market Street). Unfortunately the great ornate ventilator on the roof has been removed. This design of ventilator appears to have been one favoured by hospitals and medical facilities in the area at one time. Whilst researching for this book I was told that these two houses and the building behind all belonged to Hoylake Cottage Hospital at one time; in fact these two were owned by 'The Grand Priory in The British Realm of the Venerable Order of the Hospital of St John of Jerusalem' from an unkown date until 10 March 1947. The building behind is marked as 'First Aid Post' on the 1973 O.S. plan. All very intriguing... There is indeed one of these hospital-style ventilators preserved on the roof of a house in Beckwith Street, Birkenhead, *that* one being from the former Birkenhead General Hospital.

ON THE BEACH

NO VISIT TO Hoylake would be complete
without digging in the sand – even if you
have to keep all your clothes on! This postcard
was mailed on 18 August 1907. We are
standing at the bottom of King's Gap, at the
south-western end of the promenade. The
small turreted building on the right is shown
on the first edition of the 25-inch Ordnance
Survey plan, surveyed 1871, in the grounds
of a large house called The Gap but with no
indication of purpose – I would guess that it
was simply a summer house. The feature just
above the woman sitting on the left is strange:
under a magnifying glass it could be a small
lighthouse or helter-skelter or similar, perhaps
for the amusement of younger children? Can
you spot the lady sitting in the sand with her
knees raised? And the wheelchair? And the
boy on the left looking somewhat bemused?

THE MODERN VIEW is eerily similar, except that the people have gone home for the day and the tide has come in and smoothed the sand, waiting for their return. Each August bank holiday this patch of sand provides a temporary landing ground for microlight aircraft as part of the annual Lifeboat Day celebrations.

GOLDEN SANDS

THIS IS YET another photograph where I really wish we had a specific date, but we can at least date this photograph to within a five-year period: the promenade was completed in spring 1899 and the postcard was mailed on 17 July 1905. We are just a few yards on from the part of the promenade seen in the last photograph, the lifeboat slipway appears to be crowded with people and there are ladies with parasols on the promenade – was there an event? A more accurate date on photographs always permits more detailed

research and, incidentally, it was a detail from this card that was used for the cover of my earlier book, but I'm still not sure if the little boy had got sand in his eye or was simply just crying!

THE SHADOWS LENGTHEN as the summer sun sets in our 2011 photograph. These two ladies were simply passing on their journey and, after a little gentle persuasion, kindly agreed to pose for me, but we couldn't manage the parasol through the railings due to the netting and also due to not having a parasol!

THE 'CAR PARK'

A FANTASTIC BUT frustrating photograph! Why were all these cars parked on the sand when there was plenty of space – and no yellow lines – on the promenade? They are all facing seawards so was there a sailing event? How close was the water? The shadows suggest early afternoon, perhaps just after lunch, with a lady and a little girl leaving just as four adults arrive, in their best clothes, carrying the usual finger-trapping deckchairs. A motorcycle rests against the sea wall but the number plate is not clear. Several beach huts beyond the slipway plus a good number of spectators possibly indicate a weekend or bank holiday. In the background is the swimming pool, rebuilt in 1931, and the one penny postage means that it was posted before 1940, but unfortunately the postmark is unreadable. In the centre is the old lifeboat house with the public shelter, now long since gone, next to it. On the far right stands the Winter Gardens Theatre.

NO CARS, NO theatre, no people and no baths! The building in the distance is the new lifeboat station. Although clearly a very 'empty' photograph, actually trying to take the same view today made me wonder just how it was done – there is no slipway at that point and I doubt if anyone would bother taking a ladder. So did the unnamed photographer stand on the roof of another car or on top of a pile of deckchairs? However he (or she) did it, we owe him (or her) our thanks – the best I could manage was to perch on the railings!

ROYAL NATIONAL
LIFEBOAT INSTITUTION

THE PHOTOGRAPH ON the right
provides one of the best views of these
buildings that I have seen and it is well
worth the use of a magnifying glass.
The platform on the right still exists
and there are plans to rebuild the
shelter that used to stand there as part
of the Lifeboat Museum. The plans
also include using the Lifeboat House
with the Lookout Tower, the castellated
buildings in this photograph, which
were completed in 1899 at a cost of
£922, and the Tractor House, shown
below. Centre left is the sailing club,
completed the same year for £400. Far
right is the Lower Lighthouse, rebuilt
1865–6, last lit on 14 July 1908 and
demolished in December 1922. The
card was mailed on 9 August 1909.

THE BUILDING PROUDLY bearing the 'Hoylake Lifeboat Museum' banner is the Tractor House, which is believed to have been built in about 1930 and was designed to allow for a tractor to pull the lifeboat out to the water; the tide recedes miles every day and a tractor, ready to go, was much faster than the horses formerly employed. Due to the extreme tides, Hoylake RNLI got the first lifeboat tractor in the world. Several of the benches along the promenade have family memorial plaques on them – the one pictured here, for example, is in memory of Stephen John Liversedge, who died on 1 April 2004 aged forty-eight.

'THE FLICKS'

THE WINTER GARDENS theatre was used all year round but especially in the winter, hence the name; in the summer pierrot and minstrel shows were held on the beach, or on the bandstand further along the promenade, which is now long gone. I feel quite an affinity for this business, as *Moss's Directory*, dated 1906 and probably compiled a year or two earlier, records that the comedian William Moore, who was an integral part of the shows, lived in Hoylake, in what is now my house! The theatre later became a cinema, under the Cannon brand for many years and ending up simply as the Hoylake Cinema. This photograph was taken by Laurie Gartside on the afternoon of Monday 27 March 1995, shortly after it had closed forever.

THE OLD LIFEBOAT station lookout tower on the left and the rendered wall on the right confirm the modern photograph on the left as being exactly the same location, although an hour or two later in the afternoon! We are looking at the rear of the buildings in this view, at the bottom of Alderley Road. The new block of flats on the site is called Sandpipers Court.

BESIDE THE SEASIDE

THIS POSTCARD IS full of interesting details. It was published in Hoylake by The Handy Stores at No. 72 Market Street (now long since demolished) and was mailed on 5 September 1929. The message on the back, from 'Ada' to 'Uncle Joe', is typical of the period and concludes: 'We have been sailing and went a chara. drive last night.' The horse-drawn van on the right advertises 'Patrick's Ices – Guaranteed Pure!' and the scene on the beach is reminiscent of seaside holidays everywhere – note the piles of those infamous finger-trapping deckchairs. The shadows suggest midday and the canvases on the deckchairs show that it was breezy. The lady with the reading book has her coat fastened, so it was probably not very warm – perhaps it was early in the season?

THE MODERN PHOTOGRAPH shows a warm afternoon in the height of summer – but no one's out enjoying it! The lookout and the flagpole on the hostel, centre of the photograph, have both gone as have the railings surrounding the flat part of the roof of the house on the right – again, no one seems to want to sit out in the sun anymore! The toilet block was built and well used but is presently disused, awaiting renovation and conversion.

HOME SWEET HOME

BREATHING CLEAN SEA air was clearly seen as healthy, especially for children from inner-city areas, as Hoylake had several buildings by the sea used for this purpose, although things have

GIRLS HO

changed over the last generation. This is a closer view of the hostel on page 80. By 1923 the Ellen Gonner Home for Convalescent Children had room for seventy children, who came mainly from Liverpool. This photograph from about 1933 includes some of the female staff, one of whom can be seen standing in the doorway in the pose of pet-lovers everywhere!

INCREDIBLY, SO MANY of these flats look the same today that it was the boundary wall and the capstone on the gatepost that finally made it clear to me that it was No. 31 where the 'Girls Hostel' sign used to hang. The terracing of the front lawn has also not changed at all. These are all now private properties but they are so unchanged, at least externally, that it is easy to imagine a group of people posing to re-enact the old scene.

A COOLING DIP

HOYLAKE BATHS WAS originally opened in 1913 and was rebuilt in 1931. This view is from
a postcard mailed on 11 July 1947 and is interesting in that it shows that two-way traffic was
permitted along that part of the promenade at one time. Despite valiant voluntary efforts to keep
them open, the baths closed for ever in 1982 and were demolished in 1984. Times had changed,
people wanted warmer climes and warmer water – or at least a roof over their heads! It seems
incredible looking back, but the site stood as an empty area of rough grass for almost a quarter of a

PROMENADE AND BATHS, HOYLAKE.

century, used only on odd occasions as an emergency helicopter landing platform.

THE NEW LIFEBOAT station stands on the site of the baths – the four sections of fencing on the old photograph are the only way to accurately envisage the location as even the small slipway behind them is new. The foundation stone for the station was officially laid on 22 April 2008, not 18 March 2008 as the carving would have you believe! The facilities here are large enough to house the lifeboat with its dedicated tractor, other vehicles, changing rooms and a shop and space to walk around them. It also means that the boat and the tractor can be taken in and out as one unit, something never possible in the old building. The statue in the background is a memorial to ten lifeboat men lost at sea, eight of them on 22 December 1810; fittingly, the statue was unveiled on 22 December 2010.

ALL CHANGE

THE MORE OF these wonderful old photographs I study the more impressed I become with the photographers who achieved such excellent results; this is yet another really sharp image. It was taken from a little way up on the sandhills, which were levelled in the late 1920s or early 1930s. The area was then covered in houses. Details captured include a bathing machine (the hut on wheels) – after all, it simply wouldn't do for any gentleman to catch a glimpse of bare female flesh

– a boat riding at anchor, three smaller ones on the slipway and a fishing net draped over the railings. The wonderful ornate building in the background was the toilet block! The Queen Victoria Memorial Fountain stands tall and proud – and presumably working! The postcard was posted on 5 February 1906, which effectively dates this view to within about four years.

TODAY THE FOUNTAIN stands just as tall and twice as proud, having just been completely renovated to a really high standard, but it is, of course, illegal to actually use it! The boating pool on the left, not in existence in the earlier picture, has also just had a total makeover and repair. There are indeed also public toilets still available, in the shape of a green metal structure just behind the white wall, but please remember that they are closed in the evenings!

SLIPPING AWAY

THIS POSTCARD WAS 'Specially published for MRS. HOLMES, The Library, Hoylake' – not the library we all know and love today but a small commercial lending library in her shop at No. 10 Market Street. This was a common commercial venture in the early twentieth century. One of the boats shown in the picture at the top of page 86 seems to have been replaced by a larger boat, set the right way up – ideal for the local lads to clamber over! The little girl, on the other hand, seems more intent on getting a drink. Although this photograph is from a different series, it is of a similar age to the photograph on page 86. It was posted on 18 September 1907 but, oddly, from Sowerby Bridge to Morecambe.

LOWERING SKIES SIGNAL the end of the day in the modern photograph below, which shows the

slipway lying in a sorry state. The building of the promenade from West Kirby to New Brighton, in various stages from 1899 to 1937, certainly stopped the coastal erosion, which was measured at this point as being no less than 88ft in five years from 1895 to 1900. However, nature is not to be thwarted forever and the effects of the tide and spartina grass are now inexorably returning the beach to the sandhills from which it was formed only some 120 years ago.

SCHOOL LANE, MEOLS

MEOLS, OR GREAT Meols as it was originally called, has long since been connected with Hoylake by road, rail and sea, now forming one long but relatively narrow area of dormitory settlement. Here we are in School Lane, Meols, with the corner of Brosters Lane on the left. The gable end on the right is No. 15 School Lane and the adjoining walls and gateways are those of Hawthorn Terrace. Notice the child watching the delivery man on the right. This card was posted on 5 July 1913.

MOST OF THE trees have gone, as has the house in the distance in the old photograph. Incidentally, neither School Lane in Hoylake nor School Lane in Meols have schools in them any more! The bungalow which stands just out of shot on the corner of Brosters Lane is called The Crofton, presumably because it was built in the field recorded simply as 'Croft' on the 1845 tithe map.

GOOSE GREEN

THE BOY IN this picture is standing at the corner of Forest Road, Meols. On the right is Rose Cottage, with the gable and chimneys of Shaws Drive on the extreme right. The large building on the left is now Nos 140 and 138 Birkenhead Road. Probably the most interesting thing about this photograph, which was taken on the edge of Goose Green, is the pile of what looks like kerbstones on the grass. I suspect that these indicate that construction was about to start on Roman Road. The minutes of the General Purposes Committee of the Hoylake Urban District Council record that on 14 October 1901 they decided on the names for the new roads forming the Meols

Improvement Scheme, which were Forest, Roman, Deneshey, Hoyle and Chapel. As this photograph shows Forest Road to be at least partly built, and Roman Road just being started, it must date from about 1901.

THE TRAFFIC ISLAND has grown, but generally this scene is unchanged. The chimneys of Shaws Drive can just be seen on the extreme right, above the trees. The beautiful Grade II Listed thatched Rose Cottage is totally invisible behind the trees, which is doubly unfortunate as it is currently on sale with an asking price of £300,000; Rose Cottage has apparently been owned by the same family for some 200 years.

LEAVING
FOR
LIVERPOOL

AN EARLY VIEW of the pond at Meols adjoining the railway station – notice that at least two of the fence posts are actually in the water! The local perceived wisdom is that Braithwaite Poole, the general manager of the railway, created this pond deliberately to attract anglers in the summer (which it does) and ice skaters in the winter (which it doesn't), the idea being that these visitors would travel on his trains and thereby increase his profits. I have no idea how true the story is! The road bridge over the line can be seen in the middle distance. This view

has virtually no dating evidence in it. The photograph could have been taken any time between 1866 and 1938 but probably dates from the early twentieth century.

THIS IS AS close as it is possible to get to recreating the same view without actually hiring a boat! This view is from the far end of the Hoylake-bound platform at Meols station and the line of the main road can be seen on the left, passing the pond. The road bridge can just be seen behind/underneath the 'new' 1938 footbridge; the other buildings in the old photograph have long gone.

So, you have reached the end of your journey, and I hope that it has surprised you and maybe opened your eyes to some of what we have lost and what we have saved. In this final photograph can be seen a small group of people waiting on the Liverpool-bound platform on the right. They are waiting to board the train which is arriving to take them out of Hoylake, but not, we hope, forever!

Other titles published by The History Press

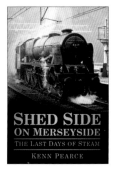

Shed Side on Merseyside: The Last Days of Steam
KENN PEARCE

Shed Side on Merseyside provides a fascinating portrait of the daily operations of the freight and passenger trains of the region during the final years of Britain's steam era. First-hand accounts from staff, including diary entries, provide an insight into this period and contemporary photographs and drawings evoke the grimy, metal-clattering, smoke-filled industry, forever etched in our industrial heritage.

978 0 7524 6048 2

Merseyside Murders & Trials
VINCENT BURKE

Notorious murders that not only shocked the inhabitants of Merseyside but made headline news across the country can be found in this fascinating book. Among them is the case of Florence Maybrick, tried and convicted for poisoning her husband in Liverpool in 1889 and the tragic story of Nellie Clarke, whose murder at Birkenhead in 1925 remains unsolved. Burke's encyclopaedic knowledge of the law and trial process is reflected in this enthralling book, which will appeal to anyone interested in the shady side of Merseyside's history.

978 0 7509 4832 6

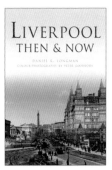

Liverpool Then & Now
DANIEL K. LONGMAN

The popular tourist city of Liverpool has a rich heritage, which is uniquely reflected in this fascinating new compilation. Contrasting a selection of forty-five archive images alongside colour modern photographs, this book delves into the changing faces and buildings of Liverpool. Comparing the fashionable man about town to his modern counterparts, along with some famous landmarks and little-known street scenes, this book is a must for anyone with an interest in Liverpool's history.

978 0 7524 5740 6

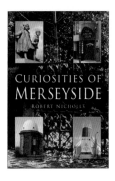

Curiosities of Merseyside
ROBERT NICHOLLS

Using over 200 illustrations, Robert Nicholls has compiled a comprehensively illustrated guide to all that is remarkable or curious in Merseyside, and over 140 curiosities of Merseyside can be found within these pages! For long-time residents of the area or for visitors this book will guide the reader to a wonderful range of interesting places to explore by car, public transport or on foot.

978 0 7509 3984 3

Visit our website and discover thousands of other History Press books.

www.thehistorypress.co.uk